Eternal Security?

Ann Maria Rowan

DEDICATION

This is dedicated to those who sincerely want to know the truth about Biblical salvation, even if it means testing and discarding erroneous teaching that they have held dear.

ETERNAL SECURITY?

Having the assurance of salvation through Jesus Christ is indeed a glorious gift from God! To know that one has been translated out of the kingdom of darkness and death and brought into the marvelous light of the Son of God is truly, *"joy unspeakable and full of glory!"*[1] The gift of eternal life in Christ Jesus is just that—a gift. Salvation cannot be earned. *"For by grace* (undeserved favor) *are you saved through faith, and that not of yourselves. It is the gift of God, lest anyone should boast."* God's gift of salvation can only be received by faith from the benevolent hand of God, who extends it freely to "whosoever will."[2]

When one receives the gift of salvation (or becomes "born again"[3]), there is a change of ownership. You no longer belong to the devil, but have become God's child. God, by His Spirit, washes your sins away by the Precious Blood of Christ[4], and writes His Law in your

---

[1]Colossians 1:13; I Peter 1:8

[2] Revelation 22:17

[3] John 3:3

[4] I John 1:7

heart[5] so that you no longer *want* to sin. He makes you alive in Christ... a new creation![6] As a new creation, you are no longer subject to following the dictates of the devil—the "prince of the power of the air."

And you has He made alive, who were dead in trespasses and sins; Wherein in time past you walked according to the course of this world, according to the prince of the power of the air, the spirit that now works in the children of disobedience: Among whom also we all had our lifestyle in times past in the lusts of our flesh, fulfilling the desires of the flesh and of the mind; and were by nature the children of wrath, even as others. But God, who is rich in mercy, for His great love wherewith He loved us, even when we were dead in sins, has made us alive together with Christ, (by grace you are saved)[7]

Before coming out of the kingdom of darkness, you were completely influenced by evil spirits. Even your thoughts were influenced by evil; you were taken captive in your mind by the devil! Your very mind was at war

---

[5] Romans 2:15
[6] II Corinthians 5:17
[7] Ephesians 2:1-5

against God and His Spirit. You were God's enemy!

And you, that were sometime alienated and enemies in your mind by wicked works, yet now hath he reconciled in the body of his flesh through death, to present you holy and unblameable and unreproveable in his sight: if ye continue in the faith grounded and settled, and be not moved away from the hope of the gospel, which ye have heard, and which was preached to every creature which is under heaven; whereof I Paul am made a minister...[8]

Amazing! Though we were once controlled by demonic spirits--following the dictates of our sin nature-- yet God freely forgives us, puts His Spirit within us and gives us the gift of eternal life! What is our part? To receive that gift by faith. We must believe that Jesus bore our sins in His body on the cross and shed His blood to cleanse us from our sin. Our old man (sin nature) was crucified with Him. We must also believe that He rose again to justify us from all our sin. By faith we receive the gift of His righteousness. We no longer walk like a sinner, because we are born again spiritually. We reckon

---

[8] Colossians 1:21-23

ourselves to be dead to sin and alive to God![9] We now are led by the Spirit of God. There is no condemnation in Christ Jesus, because we walk after the Spirit and not after the flesh![10] Does that mean we are perfect once we are born again? That we no longer sin? No. We still have the flesh to contend with. Our spirit is made new, but the flesh still has the propensity to sin. But, because the Greater One is in us, we no longer *have to* follow the dictates of the flesh. satan no longer has the right to control us. We have the authority to resist the devil and he must flee from us.[11] But… if we slip up… if we fall into sin (either by thought, word, or deed) we have an advocate—Jesus Christ the Righteous. As new creatures in Christ we do not *have to* sin. But if we do, Jesus' Blood can wash us from our unrighteousness *if we will repent of the sin*, and confess it to God:

"But if we walk in the light, as he is in the light, we have fellowship one with another, and the blood of Jesus Christ his Son cleanses us from all sin. If we say that we have no sin, we deceive ourselves, and the truth

---

[9] Romans 6:11
[10] Romans 8:1
[11] James 4:7

*is not in us. **IF** we confess our sins, he is faithful and just to forgive us our sins, and to cleanse us from all unrighteousness.*"[12]

Did you notice the word "*if*"? That is a conditional word. It does not say, "if we sin, we automatically are forgiven of sin eternally." No. It says, "*If we confess our sins*" He will forgive us and cleanse us from the unrighteousness that we have allowed into our spirits through sin. We must *repent* (that is, feel sorrow and remorse for the wrong we have done—so much so that we turn from it) and confess the sin to God for forgiveness.

Now, confession of sin is more than lip service. As a good Catholic girl growing up, I regularly went to confession. I would confess the sin of being mean to my brothers or sisters, or whatever I could think of that I had done wrong. Sometimes I didn't feel I had enough new sins to confess during the confessional time (that my sins were redundant from the last confession), so I would augment my sin list with something new (make up sins to confess to the priest). There I was, in the confessional

---

[12] 1 John 1:7-9

booth, lying about sin for which I was asking forgiveness! That was not true repentance or remorse. It was not true confession of sin, but simply lip service.

Confession of sin implies that there is heart-felt contrition—feeling bad for sinning against God. When one considers what Jesus did for us on the Cross... taking our sins in His own body on the tree—how could we lightly "crucify the Son of God afresh" with our willful acts of unrighteousness?![13] We *should* feel regret for our sins—not make excuses or try to justify our sin! If we are not truly sorry and repentant for what we have done that is displeasing to God, there is something terribly wrong with our relationship with Him. Jesus said, ***"If you love Me, keep My commandments."***[14] The opposite is true also. If you do not love Him, you will not keep His commandments. A true child of God who has received the gift of eternal life wants to please their Heavenly Father. When they sin and disappoint Him, they will want to make it right immediately and restore that relationship and fellowship with Him. Do not continue

[13] Hebrews 6:6
[14] John 14:15

in your sin! Confess your sin and repent! True repentance means that there will be a change in one's mind and behavior toward that sin. One will be so sorry for their sin that they will forsake it. As it tells us in Proverbs:

"He that covers his sins shall not prosper: but whoso confesses and forsakes them shall have mercy."[15]

In order for God to give you mercy and forgive you, you must FORSAKE sin. Stop doing it! The point of Jesus dying on the Cross and rising again the third day was to provide cleansing from our sin and to redeem us from iniquity. We are redeemed from the power of sin. Sin no longer has dominion over us, because we are now in God's grace. We are now servants of God, not of sin![16] In fact, the Bible says that if we say we are of God, but continue in sin, we are liars!

And by this we do know that we know him, if we keep his commandments. He that says, I know him, and keeps not his commandments, is a liar, and the truth is not in him. (I John 2:3, 4)

---

[15] Proverbs 28:13
[16] Titus 2:14; Romans 6:11-14

The apostle states very boldly that if we are truly "in Him" (in Christ) we will not continue in sin:

"And you know that he was manifested to take away our sins; and in him is no sin. WHOSOEVER ABIDES IN HIM SINS NOT: whosoever sins hath not seen him, neither known him. Little children, let no man deceive you: he that does righteousness is righteous, even as he is righteous. <u>He that commits sin is of the devil</u>; for the devil sins from the beginning. For this purpose the Son of God was manifested, that he might destroy the works of the devil. <u>Whosoever is born of God does not commit sin; for his seed remains in him: and he cannot sin, because he is born of God</u>. In this the children of God are manifest, and the children of the devil: whosoever does not live righteously is not of God, neither he that does not love his brother."[17]

This is pretty clear. If you are living in sin, you are a sinner—not a child of God. Remember what the true Gospel message is: "***Repent*** and believe the Gospel!" Jesus preached it; John the Baptist preached it; Peter

---

[17] I John 3:5-10

preached it; Paul preached it; and all true disciples are commanded to preach it![18] REPENT! Not just "believe." The devil believes, and trembles! But true faith in the Word of God will bring about Godly living, beginning with repentance from sin.

When one is born again, one no longer continues in a lifestyle of sin. There is a change. If one was an adulterer, when they come to Christ, they no longer commit adultery. If one was a liar, they no longer lie after being born again. If one was a thief, they no longer steal after being saved. If one was a drunkard, they no longer imbibe after receiving the gift of eternal life. If your salvation is real, there will be a change in your life. You will no longer follow the dictates of the devil, but you follow your Heavenly Father.

Far too many "Christians" bear the name, but bear no fruit. Yes... you may have put your name on the church roll. You may have had a profession of faith when you were twelve years old--but did your life change? Are you following the Spirit of God? Jesus said, *"Not*

---

[18] Matthew 3:2; Matthew 4:17; Luke 24:47; Acts 3:19; Acts 20:21

everyone who says, 'Lord, Lord' will enter into the kingdom of God, but those that DO the will of My Father in Heaven."[19]   Those who will get to enter the Kingdom of God are those who obey God's will. Your good works do not get you into heaven, but true conversion and true faith will result in a changed life… a life that is submitted to Jesus Christ as Lord, and that bears the fruit of righteousness. An apple tree doesn't have to "work at" being an apple tree. It just is. It automatically bears apples because it is an apple tree. At the very core of that apple is seed that will bear fruit after its kind. That is how it is with true Christianity. A real Christian will bear the fruit of the Spirit and do works of righteousness because they are born of God's Spirit and follow Christ. He is in them. The seed of His Word is in them, and they will bear fruit accordingly: Fruits of righteousness, not of unrighteousness.

There are people who give financially, and donate their time and talents to a church, and yet live in sin— alcoholics, adulterers, homosexuals... Why bother to put on a religious façade? You give the name of Christ a bad

---

[19] Matthew 7:21

name with your "Church-ianity." They think they are going to heaven because of "good works." They are deceiving themselves. Stop trying to placate your conscious with your "good works." They are as filthy rags in the sight of God![20] Repent if you truly are going to follow Christ. Otherwise you will end up in hell. God doesn't grade on a curve ("well, I'm not as bad as the drunkard deacon...") God's standard is perfection and holiness. And without holiness, no one will see God![21] You must be born again! You must die out to self and be wholly committed to Christ if you are a true disciple. When you are really born again, there is a change in your lifestyle. God will give you the power to say "no" to sin, and desire to live righteously.

Can True Salvation be Lost?

One might say of a professing (but sinning) "Christian", "Well, they really were never saved... therefore they live like sinners." And that is valid. Perhaps their profession of faith was just mental assent to some historical facts, but they never have truly met Jesus

[20] Isaiah 64:6
[21] Hebrews 12:14

personally. They were never born again. However, there are some who have had a true experience with God—who have actually been born-again--and yet afterwards fall back into a lifestyle of sin. Are they still saved? Is their "ticket to Heaven" really non-rescindable and non-transferable? If one is once saved, is it impossible for them to lose their salvation? Can one live like the devil and still make it to heaven? The answer is very clear. NO! And yet entire denominations espouse the "once saved, always saved" mantra (also known as "eternal security").

They are not keeping the Scripture in context. The false "once saved always saved" doctrine has damned untold millions of souls to hell with a false sense of security. That teaching makes people feel comfortable in their sin instead of fearing God enough to depart from it. It's like the deception of satan at the beginning... "did God *really* say" and "if you partake of the forbidden fruit, you will not die!"[22] We must take the whole counsel of God on a topic to be accurate. Yes... we are saved by grace through faith. But true faith will have

---

[22] Genesis 3

corresponding works of righteousness. And there are many occasions where Scripture tells us that true believers chose to "depart from the faith" and were therefore condemned.

Eternal Security Doctrine

Let us first consider why the doctrine of eternal security is believed (in spite of many scriptures that teach otherwise). There are a number of scriptures often quoted to defend eternal security teaching. When these scriptures are taken in *context*, however, they do not prove eternal security at all. When taken in context, those particular scriptures actually *refute* the "once saved always saved" doctrine. One scripture is John 10:28: ***"And I give unto them [My sheep] eternal life; and they shall never perish, neither shall any man pluck them out of my hand. My Father, which gave them me, is greater than all; and no man is able to pluck them out of my Father's hand."*** That sounds eternally secure. If you are God's sheep, you will never perish because you can't be plucked out of God's hand! THERE! Eternal security is proven! Right?? WRONG. Keep that scripture in context.

Read what Jesus said before that verse: ***"Jesus answered them…My sheep <u>hear my voice</u>, and I know them, and they <u>follow Me</u>: And I give unto <u>them</u> eternal life; and they shall never perish, neither shall any man pluck them out of my hand. My Father, which gave them me, is greater than all; and no man is able to pluck them out of my Father's hand."***

Notice that there is a condition. To be considered *God's* sheep one must **hear His voice** (which includes His written Word and the Holy Spirit's leading), and then they must **follow it.** If one is going their own way, then they do not qualify as Jesus' sheep. Only sheep (those who know and follow the voice of the Shepherd) receive eternal life. It is the *sheep* that cannot be plucked out of the Father's Hand. Sheep readily follow the Shepherd. Goats do not.

What is the Condition?

Another scripture often quoted is *"[Jesus] became the author of **eternal salvation**…"* That sounds clear. Jesus' salvation is eternal. His salvation last forever. So, if I am saved, it is for eternity. However, read the entire verse in context: *"He became the author of eternal salvation **unto all them that obey Him.**"* (Hebrews 5:9) Again, we see that there is a condition for those who expect their salvation to be eternal. It is obedience to the Lord. It means that you are now led by His Spirit, and not your own way or will. *"As many as are led by the Spirit of God, THEY are the sons of God."* [23] It is dying of your own will and way, and following Jesus as LORD of your life. True faith always has corresponding actions.

Jesus' Lordship- True Disciple

When one becomes born again, they relinquish Lordship (rule) of their life to Jesus. A true disciple of Jesus denies their self, takes up their cross daily, and follows Him. There is a spiritual change on the inside of a born-again believer. They have been set free from satan's[24] dominion and are brought into the Kingdom of God's Dear Son. They are no longer controlled by the spirit of disobedience, but by the Spirit of God. God's Spirit literally works in them "both to will and to do His

---

[23] Romans 8:14
[24] Colossians 1:13

good pleasure."[25]

As Paul writes, *"It is no longer I that live, but Christ who lives in me; and the life that I now live in the flesh, I live by the faith of the Son of God, Who loved me and gave Himself for me."*[26] One cannot follow the old pattern of sin (as one who has not been born again) and expect to go to heaven. The true *"grace of God that brings salvation teaches us to deny ungodliness and worldly lusts and live soberly, righteously, and Godly in this present world."*[27] True Christianity is not easy "believe-ism" (just belief in God). Even the devil *"believes and trembles."* (James 2:19) True faith has corresponding actions. In other words, because you *have been* born again, you will "walk the walk, and talk the talk" and desire to please God.

Saved by Works??

Just to clarify, your *works* do not save you. But your works confirm that you have been saved. Being born again results in a changed life, changed desires, and

---

[25] Philippians 2:13
[26] Galatians 2:20
[27] Titus 3:11

changed motives. Your outward actions and lifestyle manifest the changes that have been wrought in you. It is faith in Jesus' Blood sacrifice that makes us righteous before God... nothing else. It is error to think that anything that you do (good works, following church rules and regulations) can save you. If you could earn your salvation by your own good works, then Jesus died in vain. Our "good" works fall far short of God's holy and righteous standard. We must trust Jesus' righteousness.

When one receives the gift of God, eternal life through our Lord Jesus Christ, one becomes a new person spiritually. It is then that one can begin to live a truly righteous life because God's Spirit is working in them both to will and do His good pleasure. If one sins after receiving eternal life, the Spirit of Christ within them will convict them of sin. By His grace God will try to draw that one who sinned to repentance and back into a right relationship again. God is not in the business of trying to keep people out of heaven. He has done everything He could possibly do to get us *into heaven*. And we must follow the Good Shepherd to get there.

Again, there is nothing that you can DO to earn your

salvation, for it is *"by grace [God's unmerited favor] are you saved through faith; and that not of yourselves; it is the gift of God; NOT of works that any man should boast."*[28] When you receive Jesus as Lord, He imputes to you His righteousness.[29] Thank God! We are not on our own. He made the way for us to get to Heaven by His Blood and His righteousness!

New Creation

The new nature that God gives us at salvation enables us to be led by His Spirit. We are free from the Law of sin and death. We do not *have to* sin any longer. We still have the flesh, which is contrary to our born-again spirit, and wars against us daily. If we yield to the flesh and sin, God will forgive us. We must, of course, sincerely repent and confess our sin. Then *"He is faithful and just to forgive us our sin and to cleanse us from all unrighteousness."*[30] Our regenerated conscience will convict us that we have done wrong. God will graciously restore us back into fellowship with

---

[28] Ephesians. 2:8,9
[29] I Corinthians 1:30
[30] I John 1:9

Him as we acknowledge our sin and repent. He does not "kick us out of the family" for falling into sin. But if we willfully continue in sin without repentance, that's another story. If we stop following Jesus as our "Lord," we are removing our self from Him!

Blood of Sprinkling

There are areas in all of our lives that are not perfect… attitudes, motives, etc. We may not be aware of sin in our heart, but God's grace is sufficient to cover us even then. If we are sincerely following the Lord Jesus, there is an automatic covering of His Blood to cleanse us, even from unknown sins. God made provision for sin done in ignorance: *"the Blood of sprinkling."*

"And the LORD spoke unto Moses, saying, Speak unto the children of Israel, saying, If a soul shall sin through ignorance against any of the commandments of the LORD concerning things which ought not to be done, and shall do against any of them: If the priest that is anointed do sin according to the sin of the people; then let him bring for his sin, which he hath

sinned, a young bullock without blemish unto the LORD for a sin offering."

"And he shall bring the bullock unto the door of the tabernacle of the congregation before the LORD; and shall lay his hand upon the bullock's head, and kill the bullock before the LORD. And the priest that is anointed shall take of the bullock's blood, and bring it to the tabernacle of the congregation: And the priest shall dip his finger in the blood, and sprinkle of the blood seven times before the LORD, before the vail of the sanctuary."[31]

Jesus' Precious Blood

This of course is an Old Testament shadow of what the Blood of Jesus does for us. His Blood cleanses us, even when we are not aware that we need cleansing. Peter tells us that we are redeemed with the *"precious Blood of Christ…"* And we are sanctified by God's Spirit *"unto obedience and sprinkling of the Blood of Jesus Christ."[32]*

As our High Priest, Jesus sprinkles us with His Atoning Blood when we fall into sin through ignorance.

---

[31] Leviticus 4:1-6
[32] I Peter 1:2, 19

The fact that the sin is done in "ignorance" (unwittingly, a mistake), and it is not a sin of volition (a willful act of defiance and rebellion against God's Word) allows for this Blood of sprinkling to be applied for sin cleansing.

Walking in The Light

In this case, one is not willfully practicing or continuing in sin. They are walking in the light that they have of God's Word, but they have inadvertently fallen short in an area. (Isn't that all of us!) When God's Spirit reveals and convicts us of sin, we must repent and confess it to be cleansed:

"This then is the message which we have heard of him, and declare unto you, that God is light, and in him is no darkness at all. If we say that we have fellowship with him, and walk in darkness, we lie, and do not the truth: <u>But if we walk in the light, as he is in the light, we have fellowship one with another, and the blood of Jesus Christ his Son cleanses us from all sin.</u> If we say that we have no sin, we deceive ourselves, and the truth is not in us. If we confess our sins, he is faithful and just to forgive us our sins, and to cleanse

us from all unrighteousness."[33]

The true follower of Christ is walking in the light of God's Word, where the Blood of Sprinkling cleanses from all sin. When the conviction of God's Spirit shows us an area of sin (so that it is no longer a matter of ignorance), we must repent and confess it to God for forgiveness. As we read God's holy precepts in the Word of God, it is like a mirror that shows us God's holy standard, and then allows us to reflect about what is in our own heart and mind. When we see an area where we have fallen short, we need to confess and repent from it.

However, if we become rebellious and try to justify the sin revealed to us by God's Spirit, then we are not walking in the Light. Not until we truly repent and confess our sin can we be cleansed. The Blood of Sprinkling cleanses us *as we walk in the Light*.

Don't Harden Your Heart!

If rebellion against God's Word becomes a pattern—an ongoing practice of sin—then we are in grave danger of hardening our hearts toward the Spirit of

---

[33] I John 1:5-9

Truth and Grace. He is the One who convicts us of sin. By refusing to repent and follow the Spirit, we desensitize ourselves to God's working in our life. *"As many as are led by the Spirit of God, they are the sons of God."* Conversely, if one hardens their heart toward the conviction of the Holy Spirit… if one refuses to be led by the Spirit, then they no longer qualify as a son of God. God's sons are led by His Spirit.

God will not force us to love Him or follow Him. He does not leave us, but we can choose to leave Him. God's Spirit will not always strive with man.[34] If we become rebellious and refuse to follow God's Spirit… if we refuse to allow the Holy Spirit to convict us of sin, we are on *very* dangerous ground. We can actually become guilty of insulting (*"doing despite to"*) His goodness and grace. For a Christian to continue in a lifestyle of willful sin (shunning the conviction of the Holy Ghost and ignoring God's Word), then Jesus is no longer truly the Lord of their life: *"Know you not, that to whom you yield yourselves servants to obey, his servants you are to*

---

[34] Genesis 6:3

whom you obey; whether of sin unto death, or of obedience unto righteousness?"[35] If you continue in willful sin, you have become satan's servant, not God's.

Discipline for Repentance

Because of God's great love for His children, He will correct and chasten them to bring them into alignment with His will and His Word.[36] God first will patiently extend great mercy and goodness to His children to try to evoke reciprocal love, (and thereby, obedience) in them. It is the goodness of God that leads us to repentance. God may send messengers to warn His children of their error. If that does not work, He may even allow the destruction of the flesh (sickness or calamity) into a wayward believer's life to try to bring about repentance.[37] But in the end, each person must choose whether or not they are going to follow Jesus as Lord, or satan and sin.

If You Continue in The Faith…

---

[35] Romans 6:16
[36] Hebrews 12:6-8
[37] I Corinthians 5:5

Apostle Paul warns believers that it is possible for them to leave Christ if they do not continue in the faith:

Romans 11:20-22- *"Well; because of unbelief they were broken off, and you stand by faith. Be not high-minded, but fear: For if God spared not the natural branches, take heed lest He also spare not you. Behold therefore the goodness and severity of God: on them which fell, severity; but toward you, goodness, <u>if you continue in His goodness</u>: otherwise <u>you also shalt be cut off</u>."* Paul warned believers in Rome that they must *continue* in the faith of Christ, or they risked being cut off from God (as the Israelites were). One must *continue* with Jesus! The Christian life is a race that must be completed. You must endure till the end.

The Apostle further warns the Hebrew Christians that *they* could also depart from the Living God:

Hebrews 3:12-14- *"Take heed, <u>brethren</u>, lest there be in any of you an evil heart of unbelief, <u>in departing from the Living God.</u> But exhort one another daily, while it is called Today; lest any of <u>you</u> be* *hardened through the deceitfulness of sin. For <u>we are</u> <u>made partakers of Christ, IF we hold the beginning of</u> <u>our confidence steadfast unto the end</u>.*" Paul is addressing the Christian "brethren." He somberly warned them that *any of the brethren* could depart from the living God by hardening their hearts through sin. Being a partaker of Christ is contingent on one continuing to hold onto their faith. We must exhort each other, lest anyone of us depart from God through an evil heart of unbelief.

Notice that it is the sin of unbelief that causes people to depart from the Living God. It is presumptuous rebellion against God's expressed will and Word, saying that God is not trust-worthy. Doubt is a trick of the devil. One may say they believe in God, but if they doubt His Word that He *"is the rewarder of them that diligently seek Him,"* they will not diligently seek Him. If they doubt His word that *"the soul that sins, it shall die,"* they will not fear God and keep from sinning. Unbelief is the way that we depart from God. It is an insidious spiritual cancer that can get ahold of us if we are not careful. How does one guard against the sin of unbelief? "Faith comes by hearing, and hearing by the Word of God." Keep yourself in God's Word by attending a good, Bible believing church, and studying God's Word on your own. Praying in the Holy Ghost—that is in tongues – I Cor. 14:14, Jude 20--will also build your faith. (Sorry, cessationists… tongues did not end in A.D. 96!) These spiritual disciplines will strengthen your faith.

Why do you think we are admonished to forsake not the assembling of ourselves *especially as we see the day* (of Christ's appearing) approaching? Because God knew the spiritual wickedness of our day would be so rampant--like the days of Noah. Only those who diligently stay with God and guard their faith will be able to withstand the onslaught of the evil unbelief of these last days. We can get entangled in unbelief and spiritual error if we do not stay in close fellowship with God and with the church.

Paul warned the Galatians that they could get into spiritual error and fall from grace if they decided that they could *earn* their salvation by trying to keep the Levitical Law. That is the epitome of deception and pride: religious self-righteousness. It stinks in the nostrils of God, even as filthy rags![38]

"Stand fast therefore in the liberty wherewith Christ has made us free, and <u>be not entangled again</u> with the yoke of bondage. Behold, I Paul say unto you, that if you be circumcised, Christ shall profit you nothing. For I testify again to every man that is circumcised, that he is a debtor to do the whole law. Christ is become of no effect unto you, whosoever of you are justified by the law; <u>you are fallen from grace... You did run well</u>; who did hinder you that you should not obey the truth?" [39]

Here the Apostle Paul warned the Church in Galatia that they had *"fallen from grace."* He stated that they did begin right with God... they were running the Christian race well. But legalism got them entangled in error, which in turn caused them to **fall from grace**. Spiritual error (trying to be justified by their own works) resulted in their fall. But initially they *had been* right! They had received the Holy Spirit and God even worked

---

[38] Isaiah 64:6
[39] Galatians 5:4-7

miracles among them.[40] We must all be careful of error!

Paul did not take his salvation for granted. He knew that he could not afford to allow the lusts of the flesh, the lusts of the eyes, and the pride of life to overcome him. He told the Corinthians, ***"But I keep under my body, and bring it into subjection: lest** that by any means, when I have preached to others, **I myself should be a castaway**."***[41] Paul did not consider himself exempt from the perils of being rejected by God. If he would not keep his flesh under subjection to the Holy Ghost, he himself could be castaway by God.

The term "castaway" here is "adokimos" in the Greek, which means *"rejected, not standing the test, reprobate."*[42] Paul said he (*the **Apostle Paul!***) could be rejected by God as a reprobate if he did not take careful heed to his own spiritual walk. He knew that he must keep the flesh under subjection by actively putting to death the deeds of sin.[43] If the Apostle who wrote fourteen books of the New Testament under the

---

[40] Galatians 3:2-5
[41] I Corinthians 9:27
[42] Vine, An Expository Dictionary, 173
[43] Colossians 3:5-8

inspiration of the Holy Ghost, had miracles, visited the third heaven, and preached the Gospel all over the known world in his day could become a castaway, so could we!

The Apostle John was given direct warnings to the churches of Asia from Jesus Christ. These were not just for them, but were written for our admonition as well.[44]

"The Revelation of Jesus Christ, which God gave unto him, to <u>show unto His servants</u>... I have somewhat against you, because <u>you hast left</u> thy first love. Remember therefore from where <u>you are fallen</u>, and repent, and do the <u>first works</u>; or else I will come unto thee quickly, and will remove thy candlestick out of his place, except thou repent..."[45]

Did you notice this is addressing *God's servants*... the church at Ephesus? These were true Christians that initially had Christ as their first love. But then that love waned. Jesus said they had fallen away from the faith and needed to repent.

---

[44]I Corinthians 10:11
[45] Revelation 3:4, 5

Where are we in our walk with Christ? Are we as on fire as when we first came to Him? Are we spending our time in the Word and communing with Him and excited about attending church services as when we first believed? Or has our love for Christ waxed cold? We need to introspect and repent if we have left our first love.

John further (by God's Spirit) warns the church at Thyatira that they had allowed false teachers and false prophets to seduce God's servants in the church to commit spiritual fornication against Christ. In other words, the church accepted false doctrines and were not faithful to the Word of God.[46] Today MANY churches have opened wide the doors to false doctrines such as dominion theology espoused by the New Apostolic Reformation[47] leaders (aka, International Coalition of Apostolic Leaders), demonic manifestations of false signs and wonders (mysticism), worship of angels, and the false ecumenical, universalism saying one can get to God through every religion. When hundreds of

---

[46] Revelation 2:18-24

[47] https://www.gotquestions.org/seven-mountain-mandate.html

thousands of martyrs died at the hands of the Catholic church for refusing to worship Mary—doctrine matters! One doesn't kiss the feet of a priest who says, "Jesus *doesn't care* that Christians and Catholics disagree on biblical doctrine."[48] Lou Engle, what are you doing???

Jesus said, *"because you allow that woman Jezebel, which calls herself a prophetess, to teach and to seduce <u>My servants to commit fornication</u>, and to eat things sacrificed unto idols. And I gave her space to repent of her fornication; and she repented not. Behold, I will cast her into a bed, <u>and them that commit adultery with her into great tribulation, except they repent...</u>"[49]*

Jesus was very clear. You are *not* going in the Rapture with the true Church if you allow seducing spirits and doctrines of devils into your church. What about this "Judaism spirit" where people think they need to implement the Old Testament feasts and rituals to be "more holy" or "more spiritual"? DECEPTION! Repent!

---

[48] https://christiannews.net/2016/04/10/lou-engle-of-the-call-prostrates-himself-kisses-foot-of-catholic-leader-as-act-of-reconciliation/
[49] Revelation 2:20-22

Notice: these were "*My servants*" (Jesus' servants) that were seduced and deceived by false teachers. We must guard ourselves and hold fast to that which we have.[50]

Jesus tells the church at Sardis that their names *had been* written in the Lamb's Book of life, but could be blotted out unless they repented:

"hold fast, and repent. If therefore you shalt not watch, I will come on you as a thief... <u>he that overcomes</u>, the same shall be clothed in white raiment; and <u>I will not blot out his name out of the Book of Life,</u> but I will confess his name before My Father, and before His angels..."[51]

Then the church in Laodicea was warned by Jesus that He would "spew" them out of His mouth. They were in Christ... part of the body of Christ, but because they had lost their zeal for God and had become lukewarm, they would be ejected out of His Body:

"because you are lukewarm, and neither cold nor hot, <u>I will spew you out of My mouth</u>...As many as I love, I rebuke and chasten: be zealous therefore, and

---

[50] Revelation 2:25
[51] Revelation 3:5

repent."[52]

John the Revelator was given warnings to *God's* servants, the members of the seven churches of Asia. They were believers… real Christians, but most had gotten side-tracked in their walk with the Lord. Some had left their first love for Christ and the Great Commission. Jesus said they were *"fallen"* and needed to repent. If they did not, He would remove their candlestick. Those who allowed false doctrine and immorality into the church were warned that they would be *"cast into great tribulation"* if they did not repent! The Sardis church was told that in order for their names not to be *"blotted out of the Book of Life"* they needed to repent and be overcomers. The lukewarm church was on the verge of being *spewed out* of the Body of Christ! The blessings of heaven were promised conditionally in every case: *"To those who overcome…"*

In every case here the warnings are to those believers in the Church who were once right with God. They once followed their first love in Christ… They had their names written in the Lamb's Book of Life, but were

---

[52] Revelation 3:16

in peril of having their names blotted out by falling into religious apostasy, immorality, and loving the world more than Jesus. Christians can lose their position in Christ and be condemned with the world if they do not continue in the faith.

Conditions for Security

Being eternally secure with God is conditional. We do not have to worry about losing our salvation if we are led by God's Spirit and faithfully following the Lord. This is what Jesus expects of His disciples:

"My sheep hear my voice, and I know them, and they follow Me..." (John 10:27)

"For as many as are led by the Spirit of God, they are the sons of God." (Romans 8:14)

"[Jesus] became the author of eternal salvation unto all them that obey him" (Hebrews 5:9)

"Then said Jesus to those Jews which believed on him, If you continue in my word, then are you my disciples indeed" (John 8:31)

"Not everyone that says unto me, Lord, Lord, shall enter into the kingdom of heaven; but he that does the will of my Father which is in heaven." (Matthew 7:21)

Strive for The High Calling

We cannot be perfect on our own. God knows that. But as long as we are honestly trying to follow Him (walking in the light as He is in the light) we will make it. God will give us grace to help us run this race. But those who throw caution to the wind and live any way that they want to after salvation are deceived.

These Shall Not Inherit the Kingdom of God

You cannot enter the kingdom of God if you are living an unrighteous, ungodly life:

"Know you not that THE UNRIGHTEOUS SHALL NOT INHERIT THE KINGDOM OF GOD? Be not deceived: neither fornicators, nor idolaters, nor adulterers, nor effeminate, nor abusers of themselves with mankind [homosexuals], Nor thieves, nor covetous, nor drunkards, nor revilers, nor extortioners, shall inherit the kingdom of God." (I Corinthians 6:9-10)

God has a standard, and it is a holy standard. Without holiness, no man shall see God.[53] Just because

---

[53] Hebrews 12:14

man likes to acquiesce to our politically correct, immoral society and accept homosexuality and perversion as okay, it doesn't make it okay. Fornication is any sex outside of legal, heterosexual marriage. It's not okay to live with someone out of wedlock. It's not okay to watch pornography ("porneia" is the Greek word for fornication.) It may be accepted by our society, but it's not okay for Christians. Sexual immorality is not acceptable with God. Preachers… stop vacillating and saying, "Well, as long as they don't *commit the act* of homosexuality, it's okay. Let them be a celibate homosexual. They can be in the choir… they can be a deacon… they can teach Sunday School." Jesus said if you lust in your heart, it's the same as committing the act. Our thought life must be submitted to the Lordship of Jesus. Continuing to *think* sinful thoughts… lust, hate, envy, malice, can become a demonic stronghold in our mind. Then it moves into our hearts. We are to keep our hearts with all diligence, for out of the ***"heart of men proceed evil thoughts, adulteries, fornications, murders,, thefts, covetousness, wickedness, deceit, lasciviousness, an evil eye (jealousy), blasphemy, pride,*** *foolishness: All these evil things come from within, and defile the man."*[54] We are not to accept and entertain sinful thoughts, but are to actively cast them down and resist the devil. The mind is battleground where spiritual warfare is fought:

"The weapons of our warfare are not carnal, but mighty through God to the pulling down of strongholds. Casting down imaginations and every high thing that exalts itself against the knowledge of God, and bringing into captivity every thought to the obedience of Christ"[55]

Pastors, don't allow people to feel comfortable in their private sin while on their way to a devil's hell. Help them get delivered! Preach the Word so they are willing to repent of those demonic strongholds of the mind. Help them recognize sin begins in the mind, and those continual, unrepented thoughts of sin will become a stronghold for the devil in their heart. We are to cast down evil thoughts and vain imaginations that exalt themselves against the knowledge of Christ (the Word of God.) We are not to entertain those thoughts, but rather, resist the devil through the Word of God, the Blood of

---

[54] Mark 6:21-23
[55] II Corinthians 10:4, 5

Jesus and the power of the Holy Ghost.

Paul addressed the church saying "*such <u>were</u> some of you...* [homosexuals, transvestites, immoral] *but you are washed, you are sanctified...*" [56] They *were* that way but had repented (changed their mind and behavior) and had been washed by the Blood of the Lamb at salvation. They were no longer homosexuals trying to suppress unnatural lusts. They were new creatures in Christ and had been cleansed of it! They were set free by the Blood of the Lamb. You too can be free from whatever besetting sin you may have.

What about idolatry? Idolatry is not just sitting in a Buddhist temple and worshipping a stone god. Idolatry is also equated to living a party life-style. I Corinthians 10:5 tells us: *"Neither be ye idolaters, as were some of them; as it is written, The people sat down to eat and drink, and rose up to play."* If seeking pleasure is your goal in life, you are an idolater. If the big football game is more important to you than worshipping God, you are an idolater. Eating, drinking, marrying, given in marriage... that preoccupied the lives of those who didn't

---

[56] I Corinthians 6:9-11

bother to get into the ark of safety with Noah.[57] God was not their priority. Idolaters put other things before God.

It's What is in Your Heart

To sum it all up, it is all a matter of what is in your heart. Do you love the Lord your God with all your heart, soul, mind, and strength? Or have other things or other people taken first place in your heart? If you truly know Him, He will be your priority. If you have forgotten where God has brought you from, you are in danger of falling back into the world of the "lust of the flesh, the lust of the eyes, and the pride of life."[58]

Peter tells us to *make* our calling and election sure. We are to *give diligence* by adding to faith, virtue, knowledge, temperance, patience, godliness, brotherly kindness and love. If these things are in us, we will not be unfruitful in the knowledge of the Lord Jesus Christ. But if we lack these things, we are spiritually blind and have forgotten that we *were* purged from our old sins (hence, a Christian). Unless we are diligent, we can fall

[57] Matthew 24:38
[58] I John 2:16

from God.[59]

What other works of the flesh will keep one out of heaven?

"Now <u>the works of the flesh</u> are manifest, which are these; Adultery, fornication, uncleanness, lasciviousness, Idolatry, witchcraft, hatred, variance, emulations, wrath, strife, seditions, heresies, Envyings, murders, drunkenness, revellings, and such like: of the which I tell you before, as I have also told you in time past, that <u>they which do such things shall not inherit the kingdom of god.</u>" (Galatians 5:19-21)

Liquor Liberty?

I am so tired of "Christians" espousing their liberty in Christ by imbibing. A Christian does not need to be drinking alcohol. So, you have liberty in Christ to drink a little wine ("for your stomach's sake")? The wine of the first century world was not the heavily fermented alcohol of today. With all of the alcoholics in our society, why would you put a stumbling block before others who very well may have an issue with drinking? Coming

---

[59] II Peter 1:5

45

from a family of generational alcoholics I have seen the great destruction to homes and lives of those who drink.

One person I knew (a life-long alcoholic before coming to the Lord) had completely quit drinking when they became saved. Then, someone they thought of highly as being a "spiritual Christian" started drinking wine in their presence. It wasn't long before they decided it was okay to drink "a little wine," and that led them back to the bottle.

When one is drunk, they become open to demonic entities that can take over. Drunks become capable of doing horrendous things. No drunkard will inherit the kingdom of God— "Christian" or not. Keep your "liberty" to yourself, thank you!

Christians are to avoid even the appearance of evil. How do you know when you have "crossed the line" and your sip of wine becomes a habit that classifies you as a drunkard? Social drinking? Why are you trying to please others in a social setting? I thought God was the One that you should be pleasing!

"But the fearful, and unbelieving, and the

abominable, and murderers, and whoremongers, and sorcerers, and idolaters, and all liars, shall have their part in the lake which burns with fire and brimstone: which is the second death." (Revelation 21:7,8)

According to the Word of God, those who engage in sexual sin, lie, put other things before God (idolaters), murder, hate, are unbelieving or fearful, are in heresy, witchcraft, strife and envy, those who are drunkards, and the covetous *"shall not inherit the Kingdom of God."* Sorcery (and the term "witchcraft") in the Greek is *pharmakeia* (from which our term pharmacy is derived.) Taking mind-altering drugs is a form of sorcery... witchcraft. When one's consciousness is altered, it is an open door for the demonic to take up residence. Just because a drug is "legal" doesn't make it okay. The myriads of people suffering from paranoia and schizophrenia from opening the door with "just" marijuana is staggering.[60] Obviously, the harder drugs leave even a larger open door through which the demonic will happily oblige entering and occupying. Repent! Don't play with sin! Sorcerers and those into witchcraft

---

[60] https://www.medicalnewstoday.com/articles/314896.php

will not inherit the Kingdom of God. And why are you entertaining yourself with occultic books and videos? Harry Potter, anyone?? Don't you know that spirits are transferable? Keep the door to the demonic closed for your soul's sake! And your families! Parents... do you know what those video games your children (or grandchildren) are about? Do you know how much demonic witchcraft and New Age garbage spews out of them? They are hypnotizing your children's hearts and minds!

We need to watch our lives. We cannot allow ourselves to be lulled into complacency and compromise with this world. If we do, we are in danger of falling.

The Key

The key to being eternally secure is really in the attitude of the heart. Do you love the Lord because He paid for your sins on the Cross? If you truly believe that He loved you enough that He laid down His life for you, you will love Him in return. If you love Him, you will obey His Word.[61] If we remember with appreciation that Jesus purged us from our sins, we will walk in such a

---

[61] John 14:21

way that pleases Him. If we forget His sacrifice, we could fall![62]

Harden Not Your Heart

We must be careful lest we harden our hearts toward the Lord, and continue in rebellious, willful sin. Even if one has had a close walk with God, has received the Holy Ghost, and known the powerful Word of God, it is possible for *them* to fall away. If they fall into sin but refuse to repent--if they harden their heart to the Spirit's conviction--even God cannot bring them to repentance:

"For if we sin willfully <u>after that we have received the knowledge of the truth</u>, there remains no more sacrifice for sins, But a certain fearful looking for of judgment and fiery indignation, which shall devour the adversaries. He that despised Moses' law died without mercy under two or three witnesses: Of how much sorer punishment, suppose you, shall he be thought worthy, <u>who has trodden underfoot the Son of God, and has counted the Blood of the covenant, wherewith he was sanctified</u>, an unholy thing, and has done despite unto the Spirit of grace? For we know Him that has

---

[62] II Peter 1:5-10

said, Vengeance belongs unto Me, I will recompense, says the Lord. And again, <u>The Lord shall judge His people</u>. It is a fearful thing to fall into the hands of the living God." (Hebrews 10:26-31)

Notice that the writer says after one *"receives the knowledge of the truth…"* (that is, one has received Jesus, the Truth) and *"**was sanctified**,"* they could still incur the judgment of God! Sinners have never been "sanctified." This refers to none other than to believers who were sanctified by God's Spirit, but have become careless in their walk with God. They do not care that they trod under their feet the Son of God with their unrighteous acts! God shall judge His people with the fiery indignation of His wrath! That's hell!

Another frightening passage is in Hebrews chapter 6. It lets us know that one can be very spiritual, have great manifestations of God's power in one's life, ***have*** the Holy Ghost, and *still* fall away from God. Their end is to be burned. Preachers are not exempt. Knowing the Bible (but not living it) won't keep you out of hell. It is those that endure to the end that shall be saved.[63]

---

[63] Matthew 24:13

Once Partook--But Will Burn!

"it is impossible for those <u>*who were once*</u> <u>*enlightened, and have tasted of the Heavenly Gift, and*</u> <u>*were made partakers of the Holy Ghost,*</u> *And have tasted the* <u>*good word of God,*</u> *and the* <u>*powers of the*</u> <u>*world to come,*</u> *If they shall fall away, to renew them again unto repentance; seeing they crucify to themselves the Son of God afresh, and put Him to an open shame. For the earth which drinks in the rain that cometh oft upon it, and brings forth herbs meet for them by whom it is dressed, receives blessing from God: But that which bears thorns and briers is rejected, and is nigh unto cursing;* <u>*whose end is to be burned.*</u>*"* *(Hebrews 6:4-8)*

One can know God and even have His power manifest in one's life, and still be rejected and burn in hell if that one falls away from God. I personally knew a preacher who had the true Baptism in the Holy Ghost with real healings, miracles, words of knowledge, prophecy... who became rebellious toward God. He refused to repent of bitterness and hate, and thereby gave the devil an open place in his heart and mind. He continued in his rebellious attitude (even after many warnings). He felt justified for harboring those feelings of malice and hate. God finally had to give him over to a reprobate mind. He is now totally deluded and demon possessed. It's not worth your soul to hang on to hatred, bitterness, envy, or strife. That one-night stand is not worth losing your soul over. That drink or toke can send your soul to a burning, eternal hell. Don't let the devil deceive you into sinning! Repent while you can!

Departing from the Faith

Once saved, always saved? The apostles did not teach that, and neither did Jesus! In fact, the Bible teaches that in the last days many would *"depart from the faith"*! They could not depart from the faith unless they were walking in the faith.

"Now the Spirit speaks expressly that in the latter times some shall <u>depart from the faith</u>, giving heed to seducing spirits, and doctrines of devils...."[64]

Paul tells us further, that people can become lustful

---

[64] I Timothy 4:1

and depart from Christ: *"younger widows refuse* [to be put on the church charity rolls]: *for when they have begun to wax wanton against Christ, they will marry* [an unbeliever]*; having <u>damnation because they have cast off their first faith</u>... for some have already turned aside after satan."*[65]

Here the Apostle Paul says that some women who were in the faith chose to cast off their faith in Christ and to follow satan because of lust. They were no longer following Jesus. They were following satan to hell and damnation. They were once saved, but no longer.

Paul even told Timothy that *he* needed to heed pure doctrine and continue in it so that both he and his hearers could remain saved. In other words, if Timothy did not continue in sound doctrine, but departed from the faith, both he and his hearers risked losing their salvation![66]

A trap that Paul warned Timothy about was the *"love of money."* Through greed and covetousness, *"some have erred from the faith..."*[67] In other words, they were in the faith, but the love of money overtook them

---

[65] I Timothy 5:11-15
[66] I Timothy 4:16
[67] I Timothy 6:10

and caused them to err ("wander away from") the path of righteousness. Hello, prosperity preachers!

Sadly, even some of Paul's co-laborers in Christ departed from the faith! (We can't lay all the blame on preachers! People depart from Christ because they want to. Paul preached and lived the pure Gospel of Christ, and yet many of his co-workers departed from him!)

"This you know, that all they which are in Asia be turned away from me... Demas has forsaken me, having loved this present world..."[68]

The apostle also warns us in Hebrews 3:13-14 about the brethren departing from the faith:

"... we are made partakers of Christ IF we hold the beginning of our confidence steadfast unto the end..."

There's that big word "IF" again. There are conditions to your salvation. You must continue in the true faith. We are saved by faith. If one casts off their first faith, they will be damned.

James tells us that brethren (believers in Christ) can err from the truth, and must be converted back to the right way for their soul to be saved from death:

---

[68] II Timothy 1:15, 4:1

"Brethren, if any of <u>you</u> do err <u>from the truth</u>, and one convert him; Let him know that he which converts the sinner from the error of his way, shall save a soul from death, and shall hide a multitude of sins." [69]

James was not talking about someone in the world, but one of the "brethren" who was in the truth but then erred off the right path. Unless they were brought back to the path of righteousness their soul would die in the multitude of their sins.

Peter makes it very plain that leaders of the church could fall into lust and covetousness (like Balaam of old). He warns, *"if <u>after</u> they have escaped the pollutions of the world through the knowledge of the Lord and Savior Jesus Christ, they are again entangled therein and overcome, the latter end is worse with them than the beginning. For it had been better for them <u>not to</u> <u>have known the way of righteousness, then, after they</u> <u>had known it, to turn</u> from the holy commandment delivered unto them."* [70]

Peter says they were washed from the pollutions of

---

[69] James 5:19, 20
[70] II Peter 2:20, 21

sin, but fell back into the world again. He says it would have been better for them never to have known the Lord, than to know Him and then to turn from the faith. He ends his epistle warning the believers against being led astray by error and falling from their steadfastness in Christ. Peter didn't take their salvation for granted, but was compelled to warn the brethren to take heed to themselves lest they fall. We should also take heed to our walk with Christ.

Jesus said His servants should watch their lives so that they are ready for Him when He returns. If the Lord's servant does not watch their lifestyle and begins to eat and drink with the drunken, the Lord will cut him asunder and appoint him his place in hell with the hypocrites--where there is weeping and gnashing of teeth.[71] Jesus warns us to take heed to ourselves so that the cares and pleasures of this world make us unprepared for the coming of the Lord. We are to watch and pray always to escape the coming destruction.[72]

---

[71] Matthew 24:42-51
[72] Luke 21:34-36

Take Account

With these sobering scriptures in mind, it behooves all of us to take account of our own salvation with fear and trembling.[73]   Can we be eternally secure in our salvation?   Yes… if we stay close to the Lord and maintain a vibrant faith.   That personal relationship that you have with Christ will motivate you to love and obey Him, and not to engage in willful sin. Apostle John says,

*"**Whosoever abides in Him sins not**: whosoever sins has not seen Him, neither known Him.   Little children, let no man deceive you: **he that does righteousness is righteous**, even as He is righteous. **He that commits sin is of the devil**; for the devil sins from the beginning. For this purpose the Son of God was manifested, that He might destroy the works of the devil."* [74]

God's Children Are Righteous

If someone calls them self a Christian, and yet they are living a sinful life, they are not right with God. They are "of the devil." As such, they *will not* inherit God's

---

[73] Hebrews 2:3, Philippians 2:12, 13
[74] I John 3:6-8

Kingdom.

*"**Whosoever is born of God doth not commit sin;** for His seed remains in him: and he cannot sin, because he is born of God. In this the children of God are manifest, and the children of the devil: **whosoever does not righteousness is not of God, neither he that loves not his brother.**"*[75]

If one is living a sinful lifestyle (as defined by the *Bible*, not our "politically correct" society), then they **will not inherit the kingdom of God**. Eternal security is for those who walk in the light of God's Word (as He is in the Light). Then their sins are covered by Jesus' Blood.

Secure If…

In conclusion, eternal security is conditional. To say "once saved, always saved" is a false teaching not supported by scripture. The few scriptures that *seem to* indicate salvation cannot be lost, actually reinforce the fact that there are *conditions* of obedient faith if one is to remain in the path of righteousness. The just shall live by faith, and that true faith will be marked by a lifestyle of righteous living. There are many scriptures that warn

---

[75] I John 3:9, 10

believers about being "cut off" from salvation if they do not continue on with the Lord. We stand by faith. If we depart from the faith of Christ, we can fall from His grace. The New Testament has several lists of sins that one cannot engage in and expect to go to heaven.[76] We are warned that even those who once tasted of God's spiritual gifts and power can fall away from the faith. If we walk in the light of God's Word and are led by the Spirit of God, then the Blood of Jesus cleanses us. If we fall into sin, we can sincerely repent and confess our sins, and Jesus' Blood will cleanse us from all unrighteousness. One *can* be eternally secure in their salvation if they continue to follow Jesus as Lord of their life. One is eternally secure "*if…*"

Read on to learn how you may receive the gift of eternal life in Christ Jesus.

---

[76] Romans 1:28-32; I Corinthians 6:9, 10; Galatians 5:19-21; Revelation 21:8

You Can *Know* You Are Saved

You do not need to be in doubt about your soul's salvation. We can *know* that we are saved by believing in Jesus Christ.[77] Salvation is God's gift of love to you! Come to God acknowledging your sin and be willing to repent. Then believe the Gospel: ***"For God so loved the world that He gave His only Begotten Son that whosoever believes in Him should not perish, but have everlasting life."***[78]

Ask Jesus to forgive you of your sin and invite Him to come in to be the Lord and Master of your life.

"If you will confess with your mouth the Lord Jesus and believe in your heart that God has raised Him from the dead, you shall be saved. For with the heart man believes unto righteousness, and with the mouth, confession is made unto salvation... for whosoever calls upon the Name of the Lord shall be saved."[79]

---

[77] I John 5:13
[78] John 3:16
[79] Romans 10:9-13; Revelation 3:20

For additional resources, you may go to www.flwi.org.

Made in the USA
Middletown, DE
15 February 2022